Published by Jastin Enterprises, LLC

Stock Imagery supplied by iStock and Adobe

Illustrations on pages 3 and 5 by Ms. Asia Harvey

Any website addresses used in this book are fictitious, however, due to the changing nature of the Internet the web address characteristics my change since publication.

ISBN-13: 978-1542321945

ISBN-10: 1542321948

Dedication

BUILDING CYBER-READY WORKERS FROM A YOUNG AGE TO MEET NATIONAL WORKFORCE DEMANDS OF THE FUTURE

This book is dedicated to supporting the workforce needs for the 21st century in the areas of cybersecurity. Some surveys estimate that there were over 200,000 cybersecurity jobs left unfilled in 2015 and the demand will grow exponentially over the next 20 years. This book, and subsequent episodes, will educate and inspire a new generation of potential cyber technologists, workers and managers who will have had the opportunity to experience the cybersecurity territory from early childhood thus making "cyber speak" and careers in this area much less foreign.

The book targets children between the ages of 8 and 12, as well as adults who like to read with them. Everyone can benefit from reading these episodes in order to become safer online.

McGarry (2013) reported that General Keith Alexander, former Director, NSA, described cybersecurity work as a "tremendous opportunity" for young people…" He said - "This generation is coming up cyber savvy," after explaining how his almost 2-year-old granddaughter knows how to use an iPad to watch movies on Netflix. "We can train them. We can educate them."

Source: McGarry, B. (Oct. 14, 2013). NSA Chief: What Cyberwarrior Shortage?

ACKNOWLEDGMENTS

To all of my friends, family, colleagues and supporters of this effort, I thank you dearly.

~ and ~

To Roy, who fully supported all of my ideas with kindness, respect and endless love.

Jastin is twelve years old and is a very active child on the Internet. In the last episodes about Phishing, Ransomware, and Cyber Bullying, he continued with encountering the woes caused by clicking on the wrong email. This caused his family to have to pay $2,000 in ransom to an unknown hacker who took control of the family computer and taught him and the family about how to deal with a cyber bully.

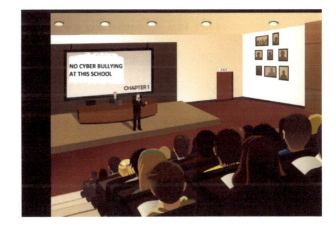

Always under the guidance of Super Cybersecurity Grandma (*Super Cee Gee*), Jastin learns a lot about being on the Internet and doing things online the right way.

Unfortunately, Jastin's cousin, "BJ", didn't listen to him or learn from the family's cyber bullying experience and was suspended from school for a whole day for doing just that!!!

1. Always be kind to others online and in- person.

2. Limit the amount of information you share about yourself and your family in the online area.

3. Cyber bullying has become very popular, so be sure to learn as much as you can about it to keep you, your friends and your family safe.

4. Encourage your school, club or church to invite an expert to talk to the students about what to do about cyber bullying.

5. Let someone you trust know if you become a victim of cyber bullying.

Even though "BJ" claimed innocence, he had to carry the "**NO Cyber Bullying**" sign every day for a full month to make up for his mistakes. Jastin and *Super Cee Gee* think that he and his buddies will finally learn a lesson!

After the previous episodes, Jastin and his family are taking steps to get closer to being safe online. But there is still a long way to go!

Just when things were starting to quiet down, after so much excitement with paying ransoms and cyber bullying, Jastin and his family decided to relax and enjoy life a bit.

Over the upcoming months, the family decided to work on fixing up the house and upgrading some of the household items that they use on a daily basis. Hearing about all the cool new gadgets that you can control from your smartphone, Jastin's mom and dad purchased new home appliances, security devices, fitness monitors and more. They decided that they would finally have a "smart house."

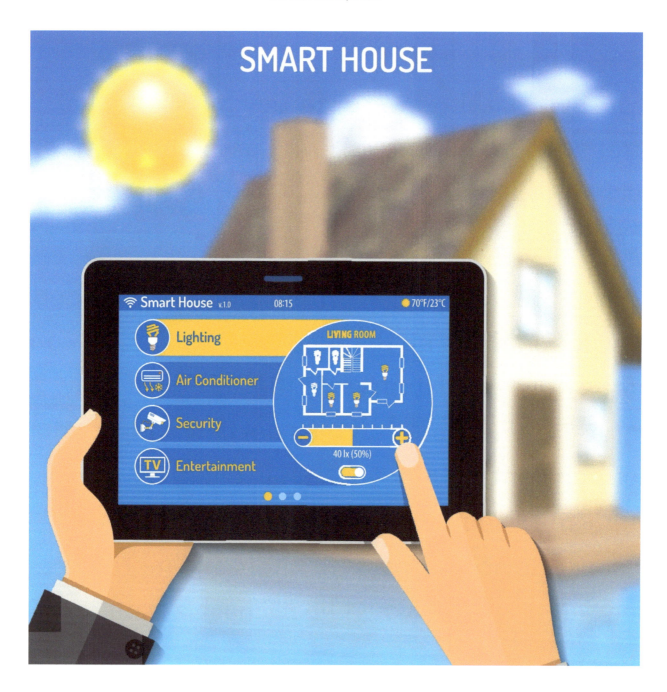

But, by far, the biggest and coolest thing was that they bought a **self-driving car** that is sometimes called "autonomous cars."

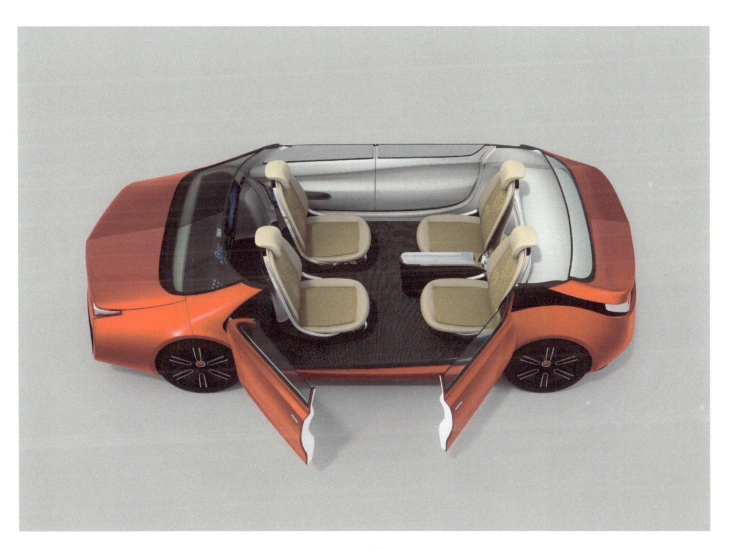

With so much new hi-tech stuff, *Super Cee Gee* thought it was a good time to talk to the family about the new craze sweeping the world called "**The Internet of Things**" or **IoT**.

The Internet of Things is a term that is used nowadays to describe the gadgets, tools, appliances, contraptions, thingamajigs, gizmos, doodads, and other machines that can connect to a **network** and be controlled through a computer or smart-phone. Not only can you control them, but they can connect to each other to transfer information to make them work better and be super useful to you.

Everyone is jumping on the bandwagon to buy these things because they are cool, convenient and can make life easier.

So, let's take a look at some of these gadgets. The first thing Jastin's family bought was a smart refrigerator. Mom loves it because there's no more calling home to Dad to see what is needed when she is at the grocery store.

The fridge keeps pictures of what's inside and Mom can see those pictures from her smart-phone while in the grocery store. The fridge also has sensors for telling you when the vegetable, egg, and milk bins are empty. And, it can automatically put a message on Mom's calendar to let her know when it's time to buy more water, milk and other stuff. **WOW, Jastin's family is too cool!!!!**

Jastin's dad is a physical trainer so, of course, he bought the entire family fitness armbands. The things you can wear that connect to computers are called "**wearable technology**."

The computer in the fitness armbands keep track of a lot of information. Everyone can know how much exercise they get, their heart rate, temperature, and even how many "virtual" steps they have climbed during the day. The family has so much fun challenging each other - and their friends - to see who gets the most exercise. The wearable watch can also keep track of things going on in the house.

Jastin's family also installed a lot of security features in their home like smart light bulbs, smart door locks, smart thermostats, and remote controlled security cameras. So now it is easy to secure the house even when Mom and Dad forget to do so before leaving.

They can lock and unlock the door, turn the lights on and off, change the thermostat temperature, answer the phone and door-bell and watch the security cameras all from their mobile phone or tablet wherever they are in the world!!!!

The coolest new IoT gadget of all was that Jastin's family bought a self-driving car.

This kind of car can travel without someone actually driving it. The family can all talk and play games while going to *Super Cee Gee's* house.

Not all of the states in the United States allow these kinds of cars on the roads, but Jastin and his family are lucky enough to live where they can own one. Their state even built special lanes for the driverless cars so that everyone can be safe on the roads and highways.

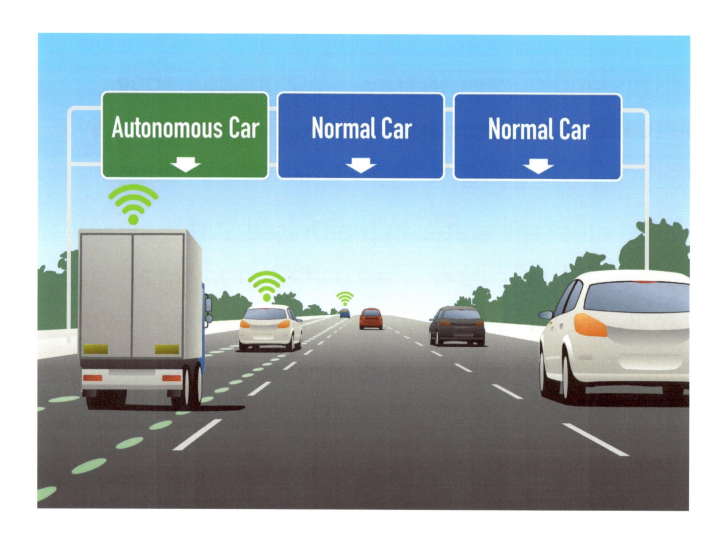

So, as you can see, the Internet of Things (IoT) is here to stay and will grow. The cool services that they bring can be very good for society. But while enjoying the pleasures, *Super Cee Gee* wants everyone to understand the concerns associated with IoT because there can be problems from many aspects.

First, there are the same old "bad" computer hackers out there who are always finding new ways to break into your network and capture your information. With all of these devices connected together, hackers can not only steal **some** of your data, but the connected devices give them access to even more of your personal stuff!!!!!

Also, the people who make the smart devices are probably collecting information about you and your family every day on how, when, and where you use the devices, so your information may not be as private as you think.

Of course, you say, "Who cares if a hacker knows that my refrigerator needs eggs?????" Yes, but your fitness and health information may be useful to someone who should not be looking at it. And the cameras in your home can be hacked by would-be burglars.

These are just a few simple ideas to think about when using IoT devices. An immediate thing to do when you purchase a smart device is to always change the **default password** that comes with it and create a new, strong password that you and your family keep private. Being aware of a few good practices can help you better enjoy the Internet of Things!!!!!

So, once again, *Super Cee Gee*, Jastin and his family are having fun with the new technologies that come along, but they are also keeping their eyes open for any cybersecurity issues along the way.

Stay tuned to the next episode where *Super Cee Gee*, Jastin and his family continue to work out the kinks in cybersecurity and learn about **Internet Privacy** and **Cloud Computing**.

Privacy is important, and if you noticed, in each episode so far, Jastin is still not being totally careful about posting personal family information... more to come on that!!!

Glossary

Cloud Computing – Everyone on the Internet or using their mobile devices today have heard of the saying putting you pictures, music, or other files "in the cloud." Simply put, this means that your pictures, music and other files are not stored or saved on the device you may have in your hand. These things are being stored by a 3rd party who hold your files in what they call "the cloud" so that (1) you don't have to use up all the space on your personal device, and (2) you can access your information from any Internet connected device. The "cloud" sounds like it is something up in the sky, but it is really a set of networks and computers that store and transmit your data.

Cyber Bullying – This term is often used to describe many undesirable activities and behaviors related to the Internet, social media, e-mail and texting. The term is derived from traditional bullying in schools, where children were threatened and mistreated in various ways. With so much use of the Internet now, the bullying activities take on a different form but the negative influences and actions are similar and more pervasive. As such, it has become very difficult to monitor and curtail. Everyone must be aware of this phenomenon so that cyber bully victims can be protected and cyber bullies can be taught to respect others.

Default Password – When you purchase computers, smart devices, and software, they often come with what is called a "default password" outlined in the setup manual. This is a general password that the manufacturer provides so that you can install and set up your technology on your network. A best practice when installing software and devices for the first time is to change the default password to your own, more personal, password or passphrase that contains a mixture of upper and lower-case letters, numbers, and special characters.

Hackers – There are many kinds of hackers, good ones and bad ones. In the past episodes of Super Cee Gee, the focus has been on the hackers who are trying to get into computers, networks, and systems for bad reasons. Hackers can be one person working out of their home or a number of people in other countries working for large governments. Hackers use their technology to break into someone else's computer, mostly to steal their information (like credit card information and passwords) to sell to others who buy the information illegally. We've learned about some of the ways (phishing and ransomware) that hackers use to get information for disreputable reasons.

Internet of Things (IoT) - In order to understand IoT, you need to know that computers communicate through the use of "addresses." Every internet device has to have this address to be located by another computer. This "Internet Protocol" (IP) addressing scheme is kind of complicated and you can learn more about that later. Today, there are many, many Internet addresses that we can associate with cars, refrigerators, alarm systems, mobile devices, light bulbs, thermostats and other things. Since these "things" can now communicate over the Internet – this term - IoT was coined. IoT is a good thing, and we easily buy and install devices because of the conveniences they provide - but with so many devices talking to each other and possibly sharing personal information, we need to think about some of the cybersecurity dangers.

Internet Privacy – Maintaining your privacy when you are online is a difficult thing to manage. Many people, young and old, freely put personal information in their social media accounts and give it online to companies from which we buy things. Also, as outlined in the Super Cee Gee "IoT" episode, some information is automatically collected by the devices we use. Online users have to be vigilant about protecting their personally identifiable information (PII) all the time.

Networks - A network is a way that you connect many computers together so that they can talk to each other. The best way to get a picture in your mind of a network is to look at the router in your house that handles your "cable" television; it gives you connections to the Internet. The router has many flashing lights on the front; in the back, it has slots or "ports" to which you can connect devices that need to get to the Internet. The router also lets computers in the house communicate. Also, the router allows you to connect devices by Wi-Fi (meaning without a cable attached). This example is just a small picture of a network. The Internet is many, many, many, many times larger with millions of computers, servers, routers and wires to make it run for people around the entire world. There's also much more to know about networks, but those concepts will be left for future lessons

Wearable Technology – This term is just what it says. It refers to items of clothing, devices, bands, hats, shoes, etc. that can be worn on a person's body and has some type of computer attached. The most popular items at the publishing of this book are fitness devices that track exercise patterns, health statistics, calories, etc. and smart watches that communicate wirelessly with other devices around you, like your smartphone or computer. Virtual Reality (VR) goggles, devices that are mounted on the head, are also popular wearable devices that allow the user to experience a 360 degree virtual world.

Matching Game

Draw a line from the concept to the right picture

Wearable Technology

Network Routers

Cyber Bullying

Cloud Computing

Hackers

Internet of Things

Privacy